Symbols, Landmarks, and Monuments

The
Capitol

Tamara L. Britton
ABDO Publishing Company

visit us at
www.abdopub.com

Published by ABDO Publishing Company, 4940 Viking Drive, Edina, Minnesota 55435.
Copyright © 2003 by Abdo Consulting Group, Inc. International copyrights reserved in
all countries. No part of this book may be reproduced in any form without written
permission from the publisher.

Printed in the United States of America

Editors: Kate A. Conley, Kristy Langanki Cannon, Kristianne E. Vieregger
Photo Credits: AP/Wide World, Architect of the Capitol, Corbis, Library of Congress,
    Prints and Photographs Division, Historic American Buildings Survey, Reproduction
    Number HABS,DC,WASH,401-1 (page 30), TimePix
Art Direction & Maps: Neil Klinepier

Library of Congress Cataloging-in-Publication Data

Britton, Tamara L., 1963-
    The Capitol / Tamara L. Britton.
        p. cm. -- (Symbols, landmarks, and monuments)
    Includes index.
    Summary: Describes the history of the Washington, D.C. Capitol complex buildings,
including the United States Capitol building, Senate and House of Representatives
office buildings, the Supreme Court, the Library of Congress buildings, and others.
    ISBN 1-57765-848-5
    1. United States Capitol (Washington, D.C.)--Juvenile literature. 2. Washington
(D.C.)--Buildings, structures, etc.--Juvenile literature. 3. Washington (D.C.)--History--
Juvenile literature. [1. United States Capitol (Washington, D.C.) 2. Washington
(D.C.)--Buildings, structures, etc.] I. Title.

F204.C2 B75 2002
975.3--dc21
                                                                2002020757

Contents

The U.S. Capitol

The U.S. Capitol is the center of the federal government. The U.S. **Congress** meets there to make laws. The Capitol is in Washington, D.C. It consists of many buildings. These buildings are called a **complex**.

Architects of the Capitol have worked on the buildings for more than 200 years. During this time, the nation and its government have expanded. The Capitol complex has also expanded to meet the needs of the citizens.

Today, the complex is still growing. Workers are building a new National Garden and Capitol Visitor Center. As the nation develops, the U.S. Capitol will continue to grow and change.

The U.S. Capitol

Fun Facts

√ Running water was installed in the Capitol in 1832.

√ In the 1840s, the Capitol was fitted with gas lights.

√ The first elevator was installed in 1874.

√ Electric lights began replacing the gas lights in the 1880s.

√ Electronic voting equipment was installed in the House chambers in 1973.

√ The *Freedom* statue on top of the Capitol is 19 and one-half feet (6 m) tall and weighs 15,000 pounds (6,800 kg).

√ It took Constantino Brumidi 11 months to paint *The Apotheosis of Washington*.

√ As many as 18,000 people visit the Capitol on any given day.

Timeline

1788	√	Maryland gives the U.S. Congress land for a federal government.
1792	√	Dr. William Thornton designs the winning Capitol plan.
1793	√	Construction begins on the Capitol.
1800	√	The north wing of the Capitol is completed.
1803	√	Benjamin Latrobe is appointed Architect of the Capitol.
1814	√	British troops set fire to the Capitol.
1818	√	Charles Bullfinch is appointed Architect of the Capitol.
1829	√	The Capitol Building is completed.
1863	√	Bullfinch's dome is replaced with a cast-iron dome. The statue *Freedom* is placed on top of the dome.
1878	√	Constantino Brumidi begins work on the Frieze of American History.
1953	√	The Frieze of American History is completed.
1958	√	The Capitol's east front is expanded.
1976	√	The Old Senate Chamber, National Statuary Hall, and Old Supreme Court Chamber are restored to original condition.
2001	√	The Botanic Garden Conservatory renovation is completed.

The U.S. Constitution

When the United States was a new nation, the U.S. **Congress** met in eight different locations. The **Founding Fathers** knew that the federal government needed a permanent home. They kept this in mind when they wrote the U.S. **Constitution**.

The signing of the U.S. Constitution

The Founding Fathers made sure land would be available as the seat of the federal government. States planned to donate this land. The piece of land could not be larger than 10 square miles (26 sq. km).

The land Congress accepted would be the seat of the U.S. government. Article 1, Section 8 of the Constitution gave Congress authority over this land.

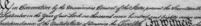

The Constitution of the United States is the world's oldest written constitution still in effect. It was signed in 1787.

District of Columbia

In 1788, Maryland donated land to **Congress** for a federal government. It could be anywhere in the state. The state of Virginia gave an equal amount of land in 1789.

In 1791, President George Washington selected some of the land that Maryland donated. This land became the District of Columbia. The landowners received 25 **pounds** per acre. Virginia's land was not used. In 1846, the federal government returned this unused land to the state.

George Washington

Washington selected **commissioners** to **survey** the government's new land. The commissioners also supervised the construction of the city and its buildings. They selected French engineer Pierre Charles L'Enfant to plan the new city. L'Enfant chose a site on Jenkins' Hill for the U.S. Capitol.

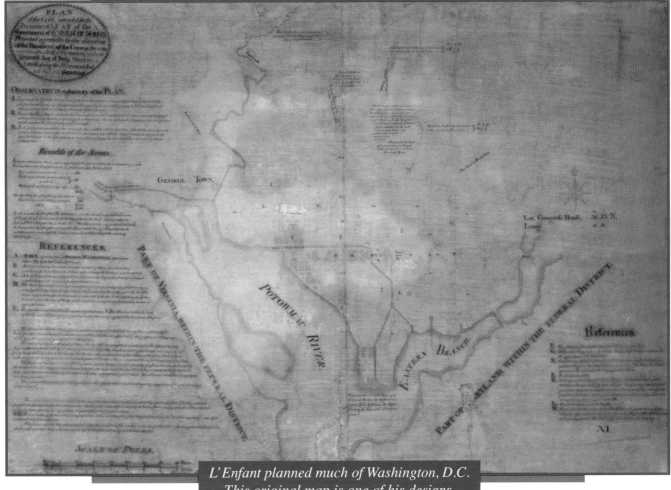

L'Enfant planned much of Washington, D.C.
This original map is one of his designs.

Choosing a Plan

The **commissioners** had hired Pierre Charles L'Enfant to design the Capitol and supervise its construction. But he would not give the commissioners any written plans for the Capitol. And he did not respect their authority over the project. So the commissioners fired L'Enfant in 1792.

That March, Secretary of State Thomas Jefferson suggested the commissioners hold a contest to select a plan for the Capitol. The winner would receive $500 and land in the new city. Seventeen plans were sent in, but the commissioners did not accept any of them.

That October, Dr. William Thornton asked if he could send in a plan. The contest had already ended. But the commissioners agreed to see his plan anyway.

In Thornton's plan, the Capitol Building had three sections. The central section had a large, rounded roof, called a dome. The other sections, called wings, were attached to the central section. One wing was for the **House of Representatives**. The other wing was for the **Senate**.

President Washington praised Thornton's plan. On April 5, 1793, the **commissioners** accepted the plan. President Washington gave final approval on July 25.

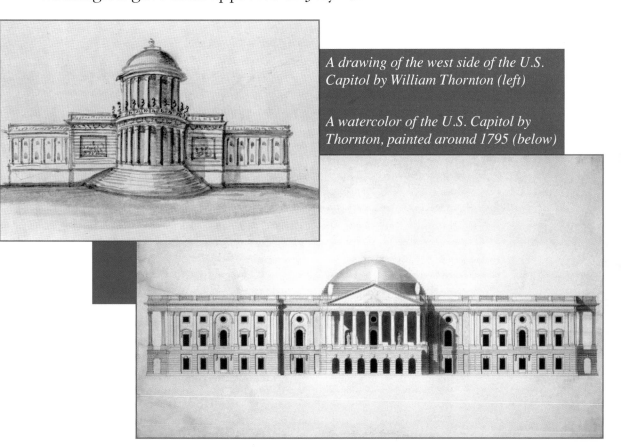

A drawing of the west side of the U.S. Capitol by William Thornton (left)

A watercolor of the U.S. Capitol by Thornton, painted around 1795 (below)

Construction

On September 18, 1793, President Washington laid the **cornerstone** of the Capitol Building. Sandstone for the building's construction was carried to the site on boats from Virginia. The Capitol construction site was in the wilderness. So finding workers who were willing to construct the Capitol was not easy.

The new government did not have much money. So the workers focused on just the north wing of the building. The U.S. **Congress**, the U.S. **Supreme Court**, the Library of Congress, and the District of Columbia's courts moved into the Capitol Building in late 1800.

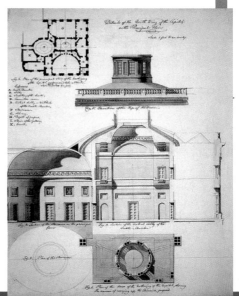

An 1814 blueprint of the north wing by Latrobe

In 1802, the **commissioners** were dismissed. A professional **architect** supervised further construction. President Thomas Jefferson appointed Benjamin Henry Latrobe Architect of the Capitol on March 6, 1803.

Latrobe designed this version of the Capitol in 1811.

Under Latrobe's leadership, workers finished construction of the south wing. It was completed in 1811. Latrobe also led the rebuilding of the north wing's interior.

Work on the Capitol soon slowed. The **War of 1812** drained most of the government's money. Then on August 24, 1814, British troops set the Capitol on fire. The building was destroyed. From 1815 to 1819, **Congress** met in a temporary building called the Old Brick Capitol.

Latrobe worked to restore the Capitol. He also redesigned the interior. But the project cost more than the government thought it should. Latrobe quit in 1817.

In 1818, President James Monroe appointed Charles Bullfinch the new **Architect** of the Capitol. Bullfinch redesigned the building's central section. He capped the building with a large, wooden dome covered in copper. In 1829, the Capitol was finally completed.

Capitol Changes

The United States continued to grow. Many new states joined the nation. By 1850, the Capitol could no longer hold all the representatives and senators.

The **Senate** decided to hold a contest for a plan to expand the Capitol. President Millard Fillmore picked Thomas U. Walter's plan.

In 1851, Secretary of State Daniel Webster laid the **cornerstone** for the new construction. Under Walter's direction, both the **House** and Senate wings were extended. Walter also replaced the Capitol's copper dome with a magnificent cast-iron dome.

Construction of the new dome in 1857

The Capitol under construction in 1864

Over the next several decades, Edward Clark, Elliot Woods, and David Lynn served as **Architects** of the Capitol. They made the Capitol larger and more modern as the United States continued to grow.

In 1958, Architect of the Capitol J. George Stewart supervised the expansion of the east front of the building. This project also included repairs to the dome and construction of a subway station under the **Senate** steps.

Architect of the Capitol George M. White made the Capitol even more modern. He added security systems and computer facilities. In 1976, workers restored the Old Senate Chamber, the Old **Supreme Court** Chamber, and the National Statuary Hall to original condition to celebrate the nation's 200th anniversary.

White retired in 1995. Alan M. Hantman became the next Architect of the Capitol. Hantman has guided the more than 200-year-old Capitol Building into the new century.

Hantman's plans include a Capitol Visitor Center and a new subway system. As the federal government continues to change, future **Architects** of the Capitol will continue to **renovate** the U.S. Capitol.

The lake in the Mall reflects the Capitol Building.

Art & Architecture

The U.S. Capitol contains many fine examples of art and **architecture**. The Capitol's cast-iron dome is perhaps the most famous architectural **landmark** in the country.

The Capitol's dome displays one of the building's best-known works of art. It is the statue *Freedom*. American artist Thomas Crawford created the statue. *Freedom* is made of bronze. It stands more than 19 feet (6 m) tall. It was first placed on top of the dome in 1863.

Many other great works of art are housed inside the Capitol Building. In the second-floor **Rotunda**, the walls display many fine works by artists such as John Trumbull.

Constantino Brumidi painted the Frieze of American History. It runs around the upper walls of the Rotunda. Brumidi created this painting by using watercolors on wet plaster. This style of painting is called fresco.

Visitors look up to view the artwork in the Rotunda.

The Apotheosis of Washington *is one of the most famous works of art in the U.S. Capitol.*

Brumidi's frieze shows famous scenes from American history. He began the painting in 1878. After Brumidi's death, Filippo Costaggini continued work on the painting. Allyn Cox completed it in 1953.

The dome's ceiling has a fresco painting called *The Apotheosis of Washington.* Brumidi painted this, also. It shows President Washington rising to heaven surrounded by many other famous people.

A collection of **murals**, located in the Capitol's **House** wing, is also popular to visit. These murals, painted by Allyn Cox, tell stories about the U.S. Capitol's history. They include portraits of the many **Architects** of the Capitol. They also show historic events, such as the burning of the Capitol by British troops.

In addition to paintings, the Capitol displays many other works of art. The Columbus Doors stand at the Capitol's main entrance. The bronze doors are 17 feet (5 m) tall and weigh 20,000 pounds (9,070 kg). They are decorated with sculptures that show the life and accomplishments of Christopher Columbus.

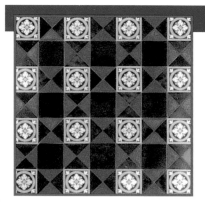

The National Statuary Hall is another famous area in the Capitol. The Hall holds statues donated by each of the states. Each state is allowed to donate two statues of notable citizens for display. The collection currently has 97 statues. Throughout the years, the statues have been relocated around the Capitol for better viewing.

The Capitol's floor is also a work of art. Minton, Hollins, and Company made the original tile flooring of the Capitol in England. The Minton tiles maintained their beauty for more than a century. In order to restore the Capitol's original beauty, exact copies are being used to replace the worn, original tiles.

A statue of Wisconsin senator Robert La Follette in the Statuary Hall

The Statuary Hall is popular among tourists at the Capitol.

The Capitol Complex

The U.S. Capitol is a **complex** with many buildings. The Capitol Building, the **Senate** and **House** office buildings, and other buildings make up the Capitol complex.

In 1897, the Library of Congress moved out of the Capitol Building. It moved into its own building, called the Thomas Jefferson Building. This was the second building in the complex, built after the Capitol. The Library of Congress buildings now include the 1939 John Adams Building and the James Madison Memorial Building, which opened in 1981.

The **Supreme Court** Building was completed in 1935. This was joined by the Thurgood Marshall Federal Judiciary Building in 1992. The House's O'Neill Building and Ford Building are part of the complex, as well.

In addition, the Capitol complex includes the U.S. **Botanic Garden** Conservatory. A new Capitol Visitor Center will be completed in 2005.

THE CAPITOL COMPLEX

1: U.S. Capitol Building
2: U.S. Botanic Garden
   Conservatory
3: Rayburn House Office
   Building
4: Longworth House
   Office Building
5: Cannon House Office
   Building
6: O'Neill House Office
   Building
7: James Madison
   Memorial Building
8: Thomas Jefferson
   Building
9: John Adams Building
10: U.S. Supreme
    Court Building
11: Russell Senate
    Office Building
12: Dirksen Senate
    Office Building
13: Hart Senate
    Office Building
14: Marshall Federal
    Judiciary Building
15: Ford House Office
    Building

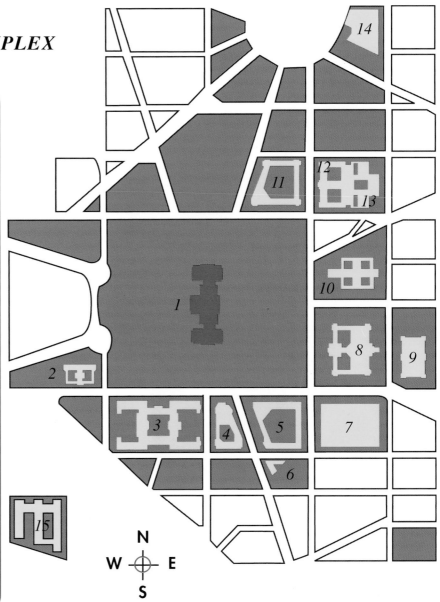

N
W E
S

The House Buildings

The **House of Representatives** gained new members as the nation grew. The representatives needed more office and meeting space than the Capitol Building provided. So construction on a new office building began.

In 1908, the Cannon Office Building was completed. It is **Congress's** oldest office building. It was named after Speaker Joseph Gurney Cannon.

The House quickly outgrew the Cannon Office Building. So in 1925, plans were begun to build a second office building. The Longworth Building was located just south of the Capitol.

Construction crews completed the Longworth Building in 1933. It is the

Cannon Office Building

smallest of the **House** office buildings. It was named after Speaker Nicholas Longworth.

In 1955, **Congress** planned for a third House office building. The Rayburn Office Building was completed in 1965. It is located southwest of the Capitol Building. It was named after Speaker Sam Rayburn.

Rayburn Office Building

The Senate Buildings

The **Senate** also grew larger as more states joined the nation. In 1901, **Congress** approved construction of the Russell Senate Office Building. It's located north of the Capitol. It is named after Senator Richard Brevard Russell, Jr.

The Russell Senate Office Building is the oldest Senate office building. Many important **hearings** have been held in its Caucus Room, such as the hearing on the sinking of the Titanic in 1912 and the **Watergate** hearing in 1974.

In 1954, construction began on the Dirksen Senate Office Building. It's located northeast of the Capitol. The building is named after Senator Everett McKinley Dirksen.

The Dirksen Senate Office Building was a modern marvel when it was constructed. It included radio, television, and motion picture facilities. It also had a telephone system, a cafeteria, and a parking garage.

The Hart **Senate** Office Building is the third Senate office building. The building began as an extension of the Dirksen Building. It provides more than 1 million square feet (93,000 sq. m) of office space. In 1982, the senators began moving into the offices.

The Titanic hearing in the Russell Senate Office Building

The Capitol Today

In December 2001, workers completed **renovating** the U.S. **Botanic Garden** Conservatory. The renovation improved the building while preserving most of its original appearance. The Palm House was also reconstructed. It rises more than 80 feet (24 m) to crown the Conservatory.

The U.S. Capitol Building Today

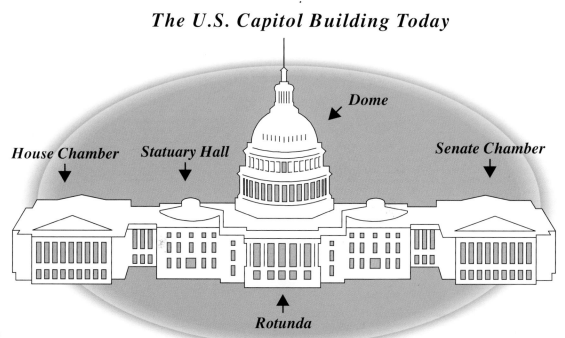

Dome

House Chamber   Statuary Hall   Senate Chamber

Rotunda

That same year, construction began on the National Garden. It will contain the Environmental Learning Center, the Rose Garden, the Water Garden, and the Showcase Garden.

The Environmental Learning Center will include teaching facilities and a library. Many kinds of roses will grow in the Rose Garden. The Water Garden will show how people, plants, and animals depend on water. Native plants of the United States will grow in the Showcase Garden.

An aerial view of the U.S. Capitol

Each year, thousands of visitors come to the Capitol **complex**. They come to appreciate its **architecture** and art. They also come to see the U.S. government in action.

To assist these visitors, a Capitol Visitor Center is being built. It will have exhibits, auditoriums, theaters, and gift shops. The project will be completed in 2005.

The U.S. Capitol is a symbol of U.S. **democracy** and government. It is an important part of U.S. history, and it is special to many Americans. This makes the Capitol one of America's great **landmarks** and monuments.

Congress meets in the Capitol to talk about laws.

The U.S. Capitol dome is one of the most magnificent structures in the United States.

37

Glossary

architect - a person who plans and designs buildings. Their work is called architecture. The Architect of the Capitol maintains, operates, develops, and preserves the U.S. Capitol and all the buildings in the complex.

botanic garden - a garden used for the education and viewing of special plants.

commissioner - an official in charge of a government department.

complex - a group of connected buildings.

Congress - the lawmaking body of the United States. It is made up of the Senate and the House of Representatives. It meets in Washington, D.C.

Constitution - the laws that govern the United States.

cornerstone - a stone at the corner of a building, often laid at a ceremony.

democracy - a governmental system in which the people vote on how to run the country.

Founding Fathers - leading figures in the founding of the United States.

hearing - the opportunity to present one's case in a court of law.

House of Representatives - the lower house in the U.S. Congress. Citizens elect members of the House to make laws for the nation.

landmark - an important structure of historical or physical interest.

mural - a picture painted on a wall or ceiling.

pound - an English coin equal to 12 shillings. Twelve shillings weigh one pound (.5 kg).

renovate - to restore or make new by rebuilding or repairing.

rotunda - a large, round room usually covered by a dome.

Senate - the upper house in the U.S. Congress. The Senate has two members from each state in the Union. They make laws for the country.

Supreme Court - the highest, most powerful court in the United States.

survey - to measure for size, shape, or boundaries.

War of 1812 - 1812 to 1814. A war fought between the United States and Great Britain over shipping rights and the capture of U.S. soldiers.

Watergate - a 1972 political crime involving President Richard Nixon. Nixon's aides broke into the Watergate Complex and tried to steal information about the Democrats. The burglars were caught and sent to jail. Nixon was forced to quit.

Show Your Colors

American flags that have flown over the Capitol can be purchased from your senator or representative. The flags come with a certificate that states the dates the flag flew over the Capitol and, if requested, a person's name or special event. The flags come in various sizes in either nylon or cotton. Write to your senator or representative for an order form.

Web Sites

Would you like to learn more about the U.S. Capitol? Please visit **www.abdopub.com** to find up-to-date Web site links about the U.S. Capitol and its construction, and the history of the United States. These links are routinely monitored and updated to provide the most current information available.

Index